CODEX: GAME OVER

A Documented Collation of the Original Ancient Egyptian
(African) Text and the Later Biblical Plagiarized Versions

Evidence You Were Never Meant To See

By Shakka Ahmose SBA

VOL I. The Pyramid Text

CODEX: GAME OVER

A DOCUMENTED COLLATION OF THE ORIGINAL ANCIENT EGYPTIAN (AFRICAN) TEXT AND THE LATER BIBLICAL PLAGIARIZED VERSION

EVIDENCE YOU WERE NEVER MEANT TO SEE

BY SHAKKA AHMOSE

VOLUME I. THE PYRAMID TEXT

CODEX: GAME OVER

The Original Ancient Egyptian Texts Used To Create the Judeo Christian Bible

Collated By Shakka Ahmose

Published by The Nile Valley Movement LLC © 2014

Foreword

The content in this book, quite possibly the first of two more to follow, was collated by my self over a period of approximately six to eight months. The entire process of reading two various translations of the Pyramid Text (both Faulkner's and Mercers') and seeking out the corresponding biblical verses took me altogether eight to nine months. I felt it was a worthy project to undertake as, from the time of my childhood, I sincerely and genuinely wanted to know just exactly from whence did the Bible come. Knowing that all religions are incapable of being honest about themselves I determined to do the requisite research, and what you are about to read, are the indisputable, unmitigated facts, in the form of documented evidence established by my self. Allow the facts to speak for themselves and do not allow the incorrect proclamations of historically illiterate, religious fundamentalists, be they so-called 'scholars', clergy, religiously miseducated relatives and, or friends (spouses and lovers included), or just plain self deluded 'believers' confound and confuse you any longer; be they on television, radio, the internet, the classroom, in a book or on a street corner, there is nothing any of them can say, do or show, that can supersede the veracity of the evidence documented here in this book. It is now an established fact that both Christianity and Judaism / Hebrewism, (hence the Bible itself) were taken directly from the cosmology and eschatological literature of ancient Egypt (Africa). The dishonest nature of just exactly how that process of plagiarism was undertaken will be covered in a forthcoming work. I give this book to you as a gift, in your effort to free yourself from religious ignorance. If you are a Hebrew then you are a Hebrew without your own religion; if you are a Christian then you are a Christian without your own religion, as all of these religions (disfigured as they are) are the rightful property of ancient Egypt and through this literary feat I, Shakka Ahmose, have given her back what is rightfully hers, 'Ma'et' (ie. 'truth'). Long Live the Nile Valley Movement.

Africa... stand up.

This book is dedicated to those Nile Valley Africans who gave this original literature of spirituality to the world in the hopes of soothing the **Ba (soul)** and **Ka (spirit)** in the face of immanent 'death'; beyond 'death' they illustrated for us... *life, life everlasting, life eternal.

Shakka Ahmose SBA, (Founder and Prime Representative of the Nile Valley Movement)

Hotep.

PS. Tell your pastors to stop lying, and to give back the money he or she took under false pretenses. God does not require your money, people do.

PPS. Eleanor, KemetAnkha Nebhu, Snt... we did it.

Because of the disparate nature of the original text, the African text

(ie. the Pyramid Text of Ancient Egypt)

there is no table of contents.

"they hasten to the place in which thou art. Thy sister Isis laid hold of thee, when she found thee complete and great, in thy name of 'GREAT BLACK.' "

Utterance 593. (Verses 1630b. - 1630d.)

THE PYRAMID TEXTS 2,400 BCE

The Oldest Religious Text on Earth

The Ancient Egyptian Pyramid Text. Originals and the Biblical Copies.

1.

A. THE ANCIENT EGYPTIAN O.R.I.G.I.N.A.L.

"Thou wilt be born (again)"

UTTERANCE 412 732b
THE PYRAMID TEXTS
ANCIENT EGYPT 2400 BCE

B. OVER TWO THOUSAND YEARS *LATER... THE GRECO-ROMAN, CHRISTIAN-JUDEO
*C.O.P.I.E.S. (*REWORKED FROM THE ANCIENT EGYPTIAN ORIGINAL):

"For you have been born again,"
1 Peter 1:23 (2nd Century CE, ie. 'A.D.')

"Except a man be born again"
John 3:3 (1st Century CE, ie. 'A.D.')

"Ye must be born again"
John 3:7 (1st Century CE, ie. 'A.D.')
NEW TESTAMENT - THE BIBLE

2.

A. THE ANCIENT EGYPTIAN O.R.I.G.I.N.A.L.

"Horus is RISEN"

Utterance 388 681a
THE PYRAMID TEXT
ANCIENT EGYPT 2400 BCE

B. OVER TWO THOUSAND YEARS *LATER... THE GRECO-ROMAN, CHRISTIAN-JUDEO
*C.O.P.Y (*REWORKED FROM THE ANCIENT EGYPTIAN ORIGINAL):

"now is Christ RISEN"

1 Corinthians 15:20 (1st Century CE, ie. 'A.D.')
NEW TESTAMENT - THE BIBLE

3.

A. THE ANCIENT EGYPTIAN O.R.I.G.I.N.A.L.

"(Osiris) who comes (again)"

Utterance 390. 684b
THE PYRAMID TEXT
ANCIENT EGYPT 2400 BCE

B. OVER TWO THOUSAND YEARS *LATER... THE GRECO-ROMAN, CHRISTIAN-JUDEO
*C.O.P.Y (*REWORKED FROM THE ANCIENT EGYPTIAN ORIGINAL):

"Jesus comes again"

1 Thessalonians 3:13 (1st Century CE, ie. 'A.D.')

NEW TESTAMENT - THE BIBLE

4.

A. THE ANCIENT EGYPTIAN O.R.I.G.I.N.A.L.

"He has received his, body"

Utterance 513 1174c.
THE PYRAMID TEXT
ANCIENT EGYPT 2400 BCE

B. OVER TWO THOUSAND YEARS *LATER... THE GRECO-ROMAN, CHRISTIAN-JUDEO *C.O.P.Y. (*REWORKED FROM THE ANCIENT EGYPTIAN ORIGINAL):

"but so that we may have our new body,"

2 Corinthians 5:41 (1st Century CE, ie. 'A.D.')
NEW TESTAMENT - THE BIBLE

5.

A. THE ANCIENT EGYPTIAN O.R.I.G.I.N.A.L.

"He is come to the Ennead, to H.E.A.V.E.N., that he may eat of its B.R.E.A.D."

Utterance 508 Verse 1116d.
THE PYRAMID TEXT
ANCIENT EGYPT 2400 BCE

B. OVER TWO THOUSAND YEARS *LATER... THE GRECO-ROMAN, CHRISTIAN-JUDEO *C.O.P.I.E.S. (*REWORKED FROM THE ANCIENT EGYPTIAN ORIGINAL):

"but my Father giveth you the true B.R.E.A.D. from H.E.A.V.E.N."

"For the B.R.E.A.D. of God is he which cometh down from H.E.A.V.E.N., and giveth life unto the world."

John 6:32 (1st Century CE, ie. 'A.D.')
John 6:33 (1st Century CE, ie. 'A.D.')
NEW TESTAMENT - THE BIBLE

6.

A. THE ANCIENT EGYPTIAN O.R.I.G.I.N.A.L.

"take this thy B.R.E.A.D., which I am G.I.V.ing thee"

Utterance 487 Verse 1047b.
THE PYRAMID TEXT
ANCIENT EGYPT 2400 BCE

B. OVER TWO THOUSAND YEARS *LATER... THE GRECO-ROMAN, CHRISTIAN-JUDEO *C.O.P.Y. (*REWORKED FROM THE ANCIENT EGYPTIAN ORIGINAL):

"Then said they unto him, Lord, evermore G.I.V.E. us this B.R.E.A.D.."

John 6:34 (1st Century CE, ie. 'A.D.')
NEW TESTAMENT - THE BIBLE

7.

A. THE ANCIENT EGYPTIAN O.R.I.G.I.N.A.L.

"[H.O.R.U.S. gives me this his B.R.E.A.D.], with which he has satisfied his subjects, and I eat of it with T.H.E.M."

Utterance 491. Verses 1058a.-1058b.
THE PYRAMID TEXT
ANCIENT EGYPT 2400 BCE

B. OVER TWO THOUSAND YEARS *LATER... THE GRECO-ROMAN, CHRISTIAN-JUDEO *C.O.P.Y. (*REWORKED FROM THE ANCIENT EGYPTIAN ORIGINAL):

"J.E.S.U.S. took B.R.E.A.D., and blessed, and brake [it], and gave to T.H.E.M., and said, Take"

Mark 14:22. 1st Century CE, ie. 'A.D.'
NEW TESTAMENT - THE BIBLE

A. THE ANCIENT EGYPTIAN O.R.I.G.I.N.A.L.

"My detestation is H.U.N.G.E.R., and I will N.E.V.E.R. eat it. My detestation is T.H.I.R.S.T., and I will N.E.V.E.R. drink it. It is indeed I who will give B.R.E.A.D. to those who exist,"

Utterance 211
THE PYRAMID TEXT
ANCIENT EGYPT 2400 BCE

B. OVER TWO THOUSAND YEARS *LATER... THE GRECO-ROMAN, CHRISTIAN-JUDEO *C.O.P.Y. (*REWORKED FROM THE ANCIENT EGYPTIAN ORIGINAL):

"And Jesus said unto them, I am the B.R.E.A.D. of life: he that cometh to me shall N.E.V.E.R. H.U.N.G.E.R.; and he that believeth on me shall N.E.V.E.R. T.H.I.R.S.T.."

John 6:35-36 (1st Century CE, ie. 'A.D.')
NEW TESTAMENT - THE BIBLE

A. THE ANCIENT EGYPTIAN O.R.I.G.I.N.A.L.S

"Raise thyself up for this thy bread, which cannot mould,"

"take the eye of Horus; thy hand is upon thy bread;"

"present thyself as thy bread,"

* "He is come to the Ennead, to heaven, that he may eat of its bread"

Utterance 497 859a.
Utterance 665b.1922 + 3 (Nt. 744). O N.,
Utterance 665b.1922 + 4 (Nt. 744). O N.,
Utterance 508 1116d.
THE PYRAMID TEXT
ANCIENT EGYPT 2400 BCE

B. OVER TWO THOUSAND YEARS *LATER... THE GRECO-ROMAN, CHRISTIAN-JUDEO *C.O.P.I.E.S. (*REWORKED FROM THE ANCIENT EGYPTIAN ORIGINALS):

"but my Father giveth you the true bread from heaven"

"I am the bread of life. Your fathers ate the manna in the wilderness, and they died. This is the bread which comes down from heaven, that a man may eat of it and not die. I am the living bread which came down from heaven; if any one eats of this bread, he will live for ever; and the bread which I shall give for the life of the world is my flesh."

John 6:32 (1st Century CE, ie. 'A.D.')
John 6:48-51 (1st Century CE, ie. 'A.D.')
NEW TESTAMENT - THE BIBLE

10.

A. THE ANCIENT EGYPTIAN O.R.I.G.I.N.A.L.S

"O Hunger do not come for me; go to the Abyss. depart to the flood! I am satisfied, I am not hungry by means of this Kmhw-B.R.E.A.D. of H.O.R.U.S. which I have eaten, which my chief woman has prepared for me, and I am satisfied thereby, I assume my (normal) condition thereby. I will not thirst by reason of Tefnet; Hapy, Duamutef, Kebhsenuf, and Imsety will EXPEL *THIS H.U.N.G.E.R. which is in my belly *AND THIS T.H.I.R.S.T. which is on my lips."

Utterance 338
THE PYRAMID TEXT
ANCIENT EGYPT 2400 BCE

B. OVER TWO THOUSAND YEARS *LATER... THE GRECO-ROMAN, CHRISTIAN-JUDEO *C.O.P.Y. (*REWORKED FROM THE ANCIENT EGYPTIAN ORIGINAL):

"Jesus said to them, "I am the B.R.E.A.D. of life; he who comes to me SHALL NOT HUNGER, and he who believes in me SHALL NEVER T.H.I.R.S.T."

John 6:35-36 (1st Century CE, ie. 'A.D.')
NEW TESTAMENT - THE BIBLE

11.

A. THE ANCIENT EGYPTIAN O.R.I.G.I.N.A.L

"for he sits of the throne of the Lord of All"

Utterance 257 v.305a.
Pyramid Texts 2400 BCE
ANCIENT EGYPT *R.O. Faulkner's trans.

B. OVER TWO THOUSAND YEARS *LATER... THE GRECO-ROMAN, CHRISTIAN-JUDEO *C.O.P.Y. (*REWORKED FROM THE ANCIENT EGYPTIAN ORIGINAL):

"he is Lord of all"

Acts 10:36 (1st Century CE, ie. 'A.D.') NEW TESTAMENT - THE BIBLE

12.

A. THE ANCIENT EGYPTIAN O.R.I.G.I.N.A.L.

"...Unas SITS DOWN on the GREAT SEAT (st wr.t) AT THE SIDE of the GOD."

Utterance 271
THE PYRAMID TEXTS
ANCIENT EGYPT 2400 BCE

B. OVER TWO THOUSAND YEARS *LATER... THE GRECO-ROMAN, CHRISTIAN-JUDEO *C.O.P.Y.
(*REWORKED FROM THE ANCIENT EGYPTIAN ORIGINAL):

".. and is SET DOWN AT THE RIGHT HAND of the THRONE of GOD"

Hebrews 12:2 (1st Century CE, ie. 'A.D.')
NEW TESTAMENT - THE BIBLE

13.

A. THE ANCIENT EGYPTIAN O.R.I.G.I.N.A.L.S.

"Thou withdrawest thyself to heaven on thy firm throne"

"Thou sittest on thy firm throne"

Utterance 483 1016a.
Utterance 424 770c.
THE PYRAMID TEXTS
ANCIENT EGYPT 2400 BCE

B. OVER ONE, TO TWO THOUSAND YEARS *LATER... THE GRECO-ROMAN, CHRISTIAN-JUDEO
*C.O.P.I.E.S. (*REWORKED FROM THE ANCIENT EGYPTIAN ORIGINALS):

"I saw the LORD SITTING upon his THRONE, and all the host of heaven standing on his right hand and
[on] his left."

"make your throne firm"

2 Chronicles 18:18 (3rd Century BCE)
Psalm 89:4 (*Dated *traditionally circa 950 BCE / New International Version ©1984)
OLD TESTAMENT - THE BIBLE

14.

A. THE ANCIENT EGYPTIAN O.R.I.G.I.N.A.L.

"take thy GARMENT of LIGHT, take thy VEIL upon thee"

Utterance 414. 737b
THE PYRAMID TEXTS
ANCIENT EGYPT 2,400 BCE

B. OVER ONE THOUSAND YEARS *LATER... THE GRECO-ROMAN, CHRISTIAN-JUDEO *C.O.P.Y
(*REWORKED FROM THE ANCIENT EGYPTIAN ORIGINAL)

"Who coverest [thyself] with LIGHT as [with] a GARMENT: who stretchest out the heavens like a
CURTAIN"

Psalm 104:2 (Dated *traditionally circa 950 BCE)
OLD TESTAMENT - THE BIBLE

15.

A. THE ANCIENT EGYPTIAN O.R.I.G.I.N.A.L.

"The HAND of Unas is come UPON YOU"

Utterance 297 v.440
THE PYRAMID TEXTS
ANCIENT EGYPT 2,400 BCE

B. OVER TWO THOUSAND YEARS *LATER... THE GRECO-ROMAN, CHRISTIAN-JUDEO *C.O.P.Y.
(*REWORKED FROM THE ANCIENT EGYPTIAN ORIGINAL):

"the HAND of the Lord [is] UPON THEE"

Acts 13:11 (1st Century CE, ie. 'A.D.')
NEW TESTAMENT - THE BIBLE

16.

A. THE ANCIENT EGYPTIAN O.R.I.G.I.N.A.L.

"Heaven rejoices"

Utterance 511
THE PYRAMID TEXTS
ANCIENT EGYPT 2,400 BCE

B. OVER TWO THOUSAND YEARS *LATER... THE GRECO-ROMAN, CHRISTIAN-JUDEO *C.O.P.Y.
(*REWORKED FROM THE ANCIENT EGYPTIAN ORIGINAL):

"joy shall be in heaven"

Luke 15:7 (1st Century CE, ie. 'A.D.')
NEW TESTAMENT - THE BIBLE

17.

A. THE ANCIENT EGYPTIAN O.R.I.G.I.N.A.L.

"They give to N. the TREE OF LIFE whereof they live"

Utterance 519
THE PYRAMID TEXTS
ANCIENT EGYPT 2,400 BCE

B. OVER ONE THOUSAND YEARS *LATER... THE GRECO-ROMAN, CHRISTIAN-JUDEO *C.O.P.Y.
(*REWORKED FROM THE ANCIENT EGYPTIAN ORIGINAL):

"take also from the TREE OF LIFE"

Genesis 3:22 (6th century BCE)
OLD TESTAMENT - THE BIBLE

18.

A. THE ANCIENT EGYPTIAN O.R.I.G.I.N.A.L.S.

"O N., thou hast [no] father, among men, who conceived thee"

"... thou who hast no father, among men, who conceived thee"

"... for thou hast no father among men who has conceived thee."

Utterance 675. v.2002b
Utterance 374. v.659c.
Utterance 412. v.728c.
THE PYRAMID TEXTS
ANCIENT EGYPT 2,400 BCE

B. OVER TWO THOUSAND YEARS *LATER... THE GRECO-ROMAN, CHRISTIAN-JUDEO *C.O.P.I.E.S.
(*REWORKED FROM THE ANCIENT EGYPTIAN ORIGINALS):

"... And call no man your father on earth"
"take unto thee Mary thy wife: for that which is conceived in her is of the Holy Ghost "

Matthew 1:20
Matthew 23:9
1st Century CE, ie. 'A.D.'
NEW TESTAMENT - THE BIBLE

19.

A. THE ANCIENT EGYPTIAN O.R.I.G.I.N.A.L.S.

"[when this hour of the morrow comes--this hour of the T.H.I.R.D. D.A.Y. (comes)]"

"this hour of the morning, of this T.H.I.R.D. D.A.Y., is come, when THOU SURELY PASSEST ON TO H.E.A.V.E.N."

Utterance 556 v.1382f.
Utterance 667 v. 1946 + 1 (Nt. 773) & v. 1941b + 2 (Nt. 773)
THE PYRAMID TEXTS
ANCIENT EGYPT 2,400 BCE

B. OVER TWO THOUSAND YEARS *LATER... THE GRECO-ROMAN, CHRISTIAN-JUDEO *C.O.P.Y.
(*REWORKED FROM THE ANCIENT EGYPTIAN ORIGINALS)

"But we trusted that it had been he (Jesus) which should have redeemed Israel: and beside all this, today is THE T.H.I.R.D. D.A.Y. since these things were done (since the crucifixion)... And it came to pass, while he blessed them, he was parted from them, and CARRIED UP TO H.E.A.V.E.N.."

Luke 24:21 & 51 (1st Century CE, ie. 'A.D.')
NEW TESTAMENT - THE BIBLE

20.

A. THE ANCIENT EGYPTIAN O.R.I.G.I.N.A.L.

"[N. rows Rē' to the west. He WRITES (THE NAME) of N. OVER THE LIVING];

"He (Rē') establishes the seat of N. ever the lords of kas; he WRITES THE NAME OF N. over the LIVING."

Utterance 584. v.15 74a
Utterance 469. V.906e.
THE PYRAMID TEXTS
ANCIENT EGYPT 2,400 BCE

B. OVER ONE, TO TWO THOUSAND YEARS *LATER... THE GRECO-ROMAN, CHRISTIAN-JUDEO *C.O.P.I.E.S
(*REWORKED FROM THE ANCIENT EGYPTIAN ORIGINALS)

"Let them be blotted out of the BOOK OF THE LIVING," Psalm 69:28. Dated traditionally circa 950 B.C.E.:
Old Testament-The Bible

"whose NAMES are not WRITTEN in the BOOK OF LIFE" Revelation 13:8. 1st Century CE, ie. 'A.D.':

New Testament-The Bible

A. THE ANCIENT EGYPTIAN O.R.I.G.I.N.A.L.S

'To say by Nut, the great, who is within the LOWER MANSION: This is (my) son, N., (my) beloved' (Utterance 3, V. 2a. The Pyramid Texts, Ancient Egypt 2,400 BCE)

"To say by Nut, the great, (who is) within the encircled MANSION: This is (my) son N., of (my) heart.Recitation by Nut the great who dwells in the MANSION..." (Utterance 7, v. 5a. The Pyramid Texts, Ancient Egypt 2,400 BCE)

"May the Eye of Horus which is in the MANSIONS..." (Utterance 81, v56b. The Pyramid Texts, Ancient Egypt 2,400 BCE. *Trans. By R.O. Faulkner)

"... and the King will not enter into Geb lest he perish and lest he sleep in his MANSION..." (Utterance 258. vs.308b. & 308c. The Pyramid Texts, Ancient Egypt 2,400 BCE. *Trans. By R.O. Faulkner)

"...he comes and goes with Re' and he has occupied his MANSIONS" (Utterance 258. v.310d & 310e. The Pyramid Texts, Ancient Egypt 2,400 BCE. *Trans. By R.O. Faulkner)

"... pre-eminent in the MANSION OF LIFE" (Utterance 297. v.440. The Pyramid Texts, Ancient Egypt 2,400 BCE. *Trans. By R.O. Faulkner)

"Horus has (?) sandals when he treads down the Lord of the MANSION..." (Utterance 299. v.444. The Pyramid Texts, Ancient Egypt 2,400 BCE. *Trans. By R.O. Faulkner)

"You are one of the two pillars of the great MANSION" (Utterance 324. v.524. The Pyramid Texts, Ancient Egypt 2,400 BCE. *Trans. By R.O. Faulkner)

B. OVER TWO THOUSAND YEARS *LATER... THE GRECO-ROMAN, CHRISTIAN-JUDEO *C.O.P.Y. (*REWORKED FROM THE ANCIENT EGYPTIAN ORIGINALS)

***"In my Father's house ARE MANY MANSIONS"

John 14: 2 (1st Century CE, ie. 'A.D.')
NEW TESTAMENT - THE BIBLE

22.

A. THE ANCIENT EGYPTIAN O.R.I.G.I.N.A.L.

"The WATERS OF LIFE which are in the sky,
the WATERS OF LIFE which are in the earth come"

Utterance 685. v.2063a & 2063b.
THE PYRAMID TEXTS
ANCIENT EGYPT 2,400 BCE

B. OVER TWO THOUSAND YEARS *LATER... THE GRECO-ROMAN, CHRISTIAN-JUDEO *C.O.P.I.E.S.
(*REWORKED FROM THE ANCIENT EGYPTIAN ORIGINALS)

"from the fountain of the WATERS OF LIFE"
"... take the WATER OF LIFE..."
Rev 21:5-7, Rev 22:17
(1st Century CE, ie. 'A.D.') NEW TESTAMENT - THE BIBLE

23.

A. THE ANCIENT EGYPTIAN O.R.I.G.I.N.A.L

"who watcheth at the Bend of THE LAKE OF FIRE"

THE PAPYRUS OF ANI
PRT EM HRU / THE BOOK OF COMING FORTH BY DAY 1250 BCE

B. OVER TWO THOUSAND YEARS *LATER... THE GRECO-ROMAN, CHRISTIAN-JUDEO *C.O.P.I.E.S.
(*REWORKED FROM THE EGYPTIAN ORIGINAL)

"...cast alive into a LAKE OF FIRE"

" ...cast into the LAKE OF FIRE"

"... cast into the LAKE OF FIRE."

".... cast into the LAKE OF FIRE."

"the LAKE WHICH BURNETH"

Rev 19:20
Revelation 20:10
Revelation 20:14
Revelation 20:15
Revelation 21:8
(1st Century CE, ie. 'A.D.')
NEW TESTAMENT - THE BIBLE

24.

A. THE ANCIENT EGYPTIAN O.R.I.G.I.N.A.L.

"Osiris A.N.O.I.N.T.S. himself with that wherewith you A.N.O.I.N.T. yourselves"

"To say: Greetings to thee, Fine O.I.L. Greetings to thee which was on the B.R.O.W. of Horus"

Utterance 473 937d.
Utterance 418. 742a.
THE PYRAMID TEXTS
ANCIENT EGYPT 2,400 BCE

B. OVER ONE, TO TWO THOUSAND YEARS *LATER... THE GRECO-ROMAN, CHRISTIAN-JUDEO
*C.O.P.I.E.S. (*REWORKED FROM THE ANCIENT EGYPTIAN ORIGINAL)

"A.N.O.I.N.T.I.N.G. him with O.I.L." James 5:14. 3rd Century CE, ie. 'A.D.': New Testament-The Bible

"for the A.N.O.I.N.T.I.N.G. O.I.L. " (Exodus 35:8. 6th century BCE,: Old Testament-The Bible)

"Then Samuel took a flask of O.I.L. and P.O.U.R.E.D. it on Saul's H.E.A.D." (1 Samuel 10:1. 6th Century
B.C.E.: Old Testament-The Bible)

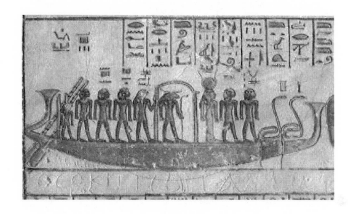

25.

A. THE ANCIENT EGYPTIAN O.R.I.G.I.N.A.L.S

"who JUDGES the words of THE GODS"

"The humans (rm.tjw) hide themselves, the GODS FLY UP"

Utterance 412. v.731c.
Utterance 302. v.459
THE PYRAMID TEXTS
ANCIENT EGYPT 2,400 BCE

B. OVER ONE THOUSAND YEARS *LATER... THE GRECO-ROMAN, CHRISTIAN-JUDEO *C.O.P.I.E.S.
(*REWORKED FROM THE EGYPTIAN ORIGINALS):

"he JUDGETH among THE GODS"

"I saw GODS ASCENDING OUT OF THE EARTH."

Psalm 82:1 (Dated *traditionally circa 950 BCE)
1 Samuel 28:13 (6th Century B.C.E.: Old Testament-The Bible)
OLD TESTAMENT - THE BIBLE

26.

A. THE ANCIENT EGYPTIAN O.R.I.G.I.N.A.L.

"... PARTS OF HEAVEN OPEN THE DOORS OF HEAVEN"

Utterance 511 1151 a.
THE PYRAMID TEXTS
ANCIENT EGYPT 2,400 BCE

B. OVER ONE THOUSAND YEARS *LATER... THE GRECO-ROMAN, CHRISTIAN-JUDEO C.O.P.Y.
(*REWORKED FROM THE ANCIENT EGYPTIAN ORIGINAL):

"... CLOUDS FROM ABOVE, and OPENED THE DOORS OF HEAVEN"

Psalm 78:23 (Dated *traditionally circa 950 BCE) OLD TESTAMENT - THE BIBLE

27.

A. THE ANCIENT EGYPTIAN O.R.I.G.I.N.A.L.

"O Osiris N., thou art the mightiest god; THERE IS NO GOD LIKE THEE"

Utterance 364 V. 619a.
THE PYRAMID TEXTS
ANCIENT EGYPT 2,400 BCE

B. OVER ONE THOUSAND YEARS *LATER... THE GRECO-ROMAN, CHRISTIAN-JUDEO C.O.P.I.E.S.
(*REWORKED FROM THE ANCIENT EGYPTIAN ORIGINAL):

"THERE IS NO GOD LIKE THEE"
"THERE IS NO GOD LIKE THEE"

2 Chronicles 6:14. 3rd Century B.C.E.
1 Kings 8:23. 7th Century B.C.E.
OLD TESTAMENT-THE BIBLE

28.

A. THE ANCIENT EGYPTIAN O.R.I.G.I.N.A.L.

"thou art the Great God, THE O.N.L.Y. O.N.E."

Utterance 592. v.1616c

The Pyramid Texts, Ancient Egypt 2,400 B.C.E.

B. OVER TWO THOUSAND YEARS *LATER... THE GRECO-ROMAN, CHRISTIAN-JUDEO *C.O.P.I.E.S.
(*REWORKED FROM THE ANCIENT EGYPTIAN ORIGINAL):

"... there is but O.N.E. G.O.D. ... there is but O.N.E. L.O.R.D. ..." 1 Corinthians 8:6. 1st Century CE, ie. 'A.D.' New
Testament-The Bible

"...the one and O.N.L.Y. L.O.R.D.. thy God is O.N.E. G.O.D." Mark 12:29. 1st Century CE, ie. 'A.D.' New Testament-The
Bible

"... there is only O.N.E. G.O.D." Mark 12:32. 1st Century CE, ie. 'A.D.' New Testament-The Bible

"... there is only O.N.E. G.O.D." 1 Corinthians 8:4. 1st Century CE, ie. 'A.D.' New Testament-The Bible

"For there is O.N.E. G.O.D. " 1 Timothy 2:5. 1st & 2nd Centuries CE, ie. 'A.D.' New Testament-The Bible

"... there is O.N.E. G.O.D." James 2:19. 3rd Century CE, ie. 'A.D.': Ne0 w Testament-The Bible

"... there is only O.N.E. G.O.D." Romans 3:30. 1st Century CE, ie. 'A.D.' New Testament-The Bible

29.

A. THE ANCIENT EGYPTIAN O.R.I.G.I.N.A.L.S

"as one who says to you your name of GREAT FLOOD which came out of She-the-Great-One ('Nut') [ie. 'Sky']"

"Unas came to his water currents which are in the land OF THE FLOOD"

"Hail to you , GREAT FLOOD, butler of the gods, leader of the SUN FOLK!

"Hail to you , GREAT FLOOD, butler of the gods, leader of the SUN FOLK!

Utterance 311 Verse 499.
Utterance 317 Verse 508.
Utterance 344 Verse 559.
Utterance 348 Verse 565.
THE PYRAMID TEXTS
ANCIENT EGYPT 2,400 BCE

B. OVER ONE, TO TWO THOUSAND YEARS *LATER... THE GRECO-ROMAN, CHRISTIAN-JUDEO *C.O.P.I.E.S. (*REWORKED FROM THE ANCIENT EGYPTIAN ORIGINALS):

"Many children were born to them after the GREAT FLOOD" Genesis 10:1 (6th century B.C.E.: The Old Testament-The Bible)

"Noah lived another 350 years after the GREAT FLOOD" Genesis 9:28 (6th century B.C.E.: The Old Testament-The Bible)

"Two years after the GREAT FLOOD" Genesis 11:10 (6th century B.C.E.: The Old Testament-The Bible) "All the nations of the earth descended from these clans after the GREAT FLOOD" Genesis 10:32 (6th century B.C.E.: The Old Testament-The Bible)

"Behold I will bring the waters of a GREAT FLOOD upon the earth" Genesis 6:17 (6th century B.C.E.: The Old Testament-The Bible)

"Then THE FLOOD came and destroyed them all" Luke 17:27 (1st Century CE, ie. 'A.D.': New Testament - The Bible)

30.

A. THE ANCIENT EGYPTIAN O.R.I.G.I.N.A.L.S

"so HE (the deceased) TAKES HIS PLACE AT THE T.A.B.L.E. (PARTAKES OF HIS M.E.A.L.), since T.H.E.Y. are SATISFIED WITH THEIR N.O.U.R.I.S.H.M.E.N.T. (contentment)."

"LORD of the five MEALS, three in heaven, two ON EARTH."

Utterance 406. 708c., Utterance 409. 717b.
THE PYRAMID TEXTS
ANCIENT EGYPT 2,400 BCE

B. OVER TWO THOUSAND YEARS *LATER... THE GRECO-ROMAN, CHRISTIAN-JUDEO *C.O.P.Y (*REWORKED FROM THE ANCIENT EGYPTIAN ORIGINALS):

"...T.H.E.Y. ... shared in THE LORD'S S.U.P.P.E.R., and A.T.E. T.O.G.E.T.H.E.R."

Luke 17:27. 1st Century CE, ie. 'A.D.'
NEW TESTAMENT - THE BIBLE

31.

A. THE ANCIENT EGYPTIAN O.R.I.G.I.N.A.L.S

"...MY... SON... WITH WHO I AM WELL PLEASED"

"... MY BELOVED SON... WITH WHOM HE IS WELL PLEASED"

Utterance 1, Utterance 3
THE PYRAMID TEXTS (*R.O. Faulkner's trans.)
ANCIENT EGYPT 2,400 BCE

B. OVER TWO THOUSAND YEARS *LATER... THE GRECO-ROMAN, CHRISTIAN-JUDEO *C.O.P.I.E.S.
(*REWORKED FROM THE ANCIENT EGYPTIAN ORIGINALS):

"This is MY BELOVED SON, in WHOM I AM WELL PLEASED"
"...MY BELOVED SON, in WHOM I AM WELL PLEASED"
Matthew 3:17. 1st Century CE, ie. 'A.D.':
Mark 1:11. 1st Century CE, ie. 'A.D.'

NEW TESTAMENT-THE BIBLE

32.

A. THE ANCIENT EGYPTIAN O.R.I.G.I.N.A.L.

"N.[ie. 'OSIRIS'] IS CONCEIVED BY RE' [ie. 'CONCEIVED BY GOD']; HE IS BORN OF RE' [ie. 'BORN OF GOD'],
N.[ie. 'OSIRIS'] IS THY SEED, O RE'[ie. 'THY SEED OF GOD'], the [AP]POINTED, IN HIS NAME OF 'HORUS...'

Utterance 576. 1508b.-1508c.
THE PYRAMID TEXTS
ANCIENT EGYPT 2,400 BCE

B. OVER ONE, TO TWO THOUSAND YEARS *LATER... THE GRECO-ROMAN, CHRISTIAN-JUDEO
*C.O.P.I.E.S. (*REWORKED FROM THE ANCIENT EGYPTIAN ORIGINALS):

"the CHRIST IS BORN OF GOD" 1 John 5:1. 1st Century CE, ie. 'A.D.': New Testament - The Bible

"GOD SENT HIS SON" Galatians 4:4. 1st Century CE, ie. 'A.D.': New Testament - The Bible

"And what doth one seek, but THE SEED OF GOD" Malachi 2:15. 5th Century B.C.E.: Old Testament –The
Bible

33.

A. THE ANCIENT EGYPTIAN O.R.I.G.I.N.A.L.

"... the watchers of Buto AP.P.O.I.N.T.E.D. HIM, and the watchers of Hierakonpolis P.R.O.C.L.A.I.M.E.D. HIM"
Utterance 483. V.1013a.
THE PYRAMID TEXTS (*R.O. Faulkner's trans.)
ANCIENT EGYPT 2,400 BCE

B. OVER TWO THOUSAND YEARS *LATER... THE GRECO-ROMAN, CHRISTIAN-JUDEO *C.O.P.I.E.S.
(*REWORKED FROM THE ANCIENT EGYPTIAN ORIGINAL):

"This child (ie. 'Jesus') is A.P.P.O.I.N.T.E.D." Luke 2:34. 1st Century CE, ie. 'A.D.': New Testament - The
Bible

"he P.R.O.C.L.A.I.M.E.D. the Christ..." Acts 9:20. 1st Century CE, ie. 'A.D.': New Testament - The Bible

34.

A. THE ANCIENT EGYPTIAN O.R.I.G.I.N.A.L.S

""O OSIRIS... in YOUR NAME OF GOD"

"... in thy NAME OF 'GOD' "

Utterance 33 *R.O. Faulkner's trans.
Utterance 356. vs.580b.
Utterance 366 vs.630c.
THE PYRAMID TEXTS (*R.O. Faulkner's trans.)
ANCIENT EGYPT 2,400 BCE

B. OVER ONE THOUSAND YEARS *LATER... THE GRECO-ROMAN, CHRISTIAN-JUDEO *C.O.P.Y.
(*REWORKED FROM THE ANCIENT EGYPTIAN ORIGINALS):

"According to THY NAME, O GOD,"

Psalm 48:10 (*Dated *traditionally circa 950 BCE
OLD TESTAMENT-THE BIBLE

35.

A. THE ANCIENT EGYPTIAN O.R.I.G.I.N.A.L.S

"as for OSIRIS IN HIS SUFFERING"

"laments for thee, as for OSIRIS IN HIS SUFFERING."

Utterance 461 872c.
Utterance 466 884b.
THE PYRAMID TEXTS (*R.O. Faulkner's trans.)
ANCIENT EGYPT 2,400 BCE

B. OVER TWO THOUSAND YEARS *LATER... THE GRECO-ROMAN, CHRISTIAN-JUDEO *C.O.P.I.E.S.
(*REWORKED FROM THE ANCIENT EGYPTIAN ORIGINALS):

"as Christ HATH SUFFERED"

"For Christ also hath once SUFFERED"

"For as the SUFFERINGS OF CHRIST"

1 Peter 4:1
1 Peter 3:18
2 Corinthians 1:5
1st Century CE, ie. 'A.D.'
NEW TESTAMENT-THE BIBLE

A. THE ANCIENT EGYPTIAN O.R.I.G.I.N.A.L.S

"Horus, LORD OF HEAVEN"

"N. comes to thee, LORD OF HEAVEN; N. comes to thee, OSIRIS"

"N. comes to thee, LORD OF HEAVEN; N. comes to thee, Osiris

"N. comes to thee, LORD OF HEAVEN; N. comes to thee, Osiris,

Utterance 461 872c.
Utterance 466 884b.
Utterance 477 964a
Utterance 477 966a.
THE PYRAMID TEXTS (*R.O. Faulkner's trans.)
ANCIENT EGYPT 2,400 BCE

B. OVER TWO THOUSAND YEARS *LATER... THE GRECO-ROMAN, CHRISTIAN-JUDEO *C.O.P.I.E.S.
(*REWORKED FROM THE ANCIENT EGYPTIAN ORIGINALS):

"he is LORD OF HEAVEN"

"LORD OF HEAVEN"

Acts 17:24
Matthew 11:25
1st Century CE, ie. 'A.D.'
NEW TESTAMENT-THE BIBLE

37.

A. THE ANCIENT EGYPTIAN O.R.I.G.I.N.A.L.S

"Homage to thee, KING OF KINGS, AND LORD OF LORDS, and PRINCE OF PRINCES."

From: HYMN TO OSIRIS UN-NEFER
THE PAPYRUS OF ANI
PRT EM HRU / THE BOOK OF COMING FORTH BY DAY 1250 BCE

B. OVER ONE THOUSAND YEARS *LATER... THE GRECO-ROMAN, CHRISTIAN-JUDEO *C.O.P.I.E.S.
(*REWORKED FROM THE ANCIENT EGYPTIAN ORIGINALS):

"the KING OF KINGS, AND LORD OF LORDS" 1 Timothy 6:15. 1st Century CE, ie. 'A.D.'

"KING OF KINGS, AND LORD OF LORDS" Revelation 19:16. 1st Century CE, ie. 'A.D.'

"for he is LORD OF LORD AND KING OF KINGS" Revelation 17:14. 1st Century CE, ie. 'A.D.'

"Thou, O king, [art] a KING OF KINGS" Daniel 2:37. 2nd Century B.C.E.: Old Testament-The Bible

"... the PRINCE OF PRINCES" Daniel 8:25. 2nd Century B.C.E.: Old Testament-The Bible

38.

A. THE ANCIENT EGYPTIAN O.R.I.G.I.N.A.L.

" To thee come THE WISE AND THE UNDERSTANDING"

Utterance 676. v.2017a.
THE PYRAMID TEXTS
ANCIENT EGYPT 2,400 BCE

B. OVER TWO THOUSAND YEARS *LATER... THE GRECO-ROMAN, CHRISTIAN-JUDEO *C.O.P.Y.
(*REWORKED FROM THE ANCIENT EGYPTIAN ORIGINAL):

"behold, there came WISE MEN"

Matthew 2:1
1st Century CE, ie. 'A.D.' NEW TESTAMENT-THE BIBLE

39.

A. THE ANCIENT EGYPTIAN O.R.I.G.I.N.A.L.

"The *S.E.R.P.E.N.T., 'Fowling-with-the-phallus', Horus has SMASHED IT'S *M.O.U.T.H. with his foot (or, sole of his foot).

Utterance 388. v.681d-v.681e..
THE PYRAMID TEXTS
ANCIENT EGYPT 2,400 BCE

B. ALMOST TWO THOUSAND YEARS *LATER... THE GRECO-ROMAN, CHRISTIAN-JUDEO *C.O.P.Y.. (*REWORKED FROM THE ANCIENT EGYPTIAN ORIGINAL):

"And the *S.E.R.P.E.N.T. *S.A.I.D. unto ..."

GENESIS 3:4. 6th century B.C.E.
OLD TESTAMENT-THE BIBLE

40.

A. THE ANCIENT EGYPTIAN O.R.I.G.I.N.A.L.

"N. was given birth by his father Atum, BEFORE THE SKY CAME INTO BEING, BEFORE THE EARTH CAME INTO BEING, BEFORE MEN CAME INTO BEING, BEFORE THE GODS WERE BORN, BEFORE DEATH CAME INTO BEING.

Utterance 572. v.1466B.-v.1466D.
THE PYRAMID TEXTS
ANCIENT EGYPT 2,400 BCE

B. OVER TWO THOUSAND YEARS *LATER... THE GRECO-ROMAN, CHRISTIAN-JUDEO *C.O.P.I.E.S. (*REWORKED FROM THE ANCIENT EGYPTIAN ORIGINALS):

""Yahweh created me at the beginning of his work, the first of his acts of old. Ages ago I was set up, at the first, BEFORE THE BEGINNING OF THE EARTH. WHEN THERE WERE NO DEPTHS I WAS BROUGHT FORTH, WHEN THERE WERE NO SPRINGS ABUNDANT WITH WATER. BEFORE THE MOUNTAINS HAD BEEN SHAPED, BEFORE THE HILLS, I WAS BROUGHT FORTH"

Proverbs 8:22-30. Dated *traditionally circa 950 BCE
OLD TESTAMENT - THE BIBLE

41.

A. THE ANCIENT EGYPTIAN O.R.I.G.I.N.A.L.S.

"O, M.O.R.N.I.N.G. S.T.A.R., Horus of the D⬚.t,"

"He appoints thee as THE M.O.R.N.I.N.G. S.T.A.R. ... and thou sittest upon thy throne."

"He appoints thee as THE M.O.R.N.I.N.G. S.T.A.R."

"thou ascendest (or, goest forth) as THE M.O.R.N.I.N.G. S.T.A.R."

"when thou ascendest as a star, as THE M.O.R.N.I.N.G. S.T.A.R."

Utterance 519. v.1207a.
Utterance 437. v.805a-v.805.b
Utterance 610. v.1719f.
Utterance 461. v.871b.
Utterance 676. v.2014b.
THE PYRAMID TEXTS
ANCIENT EGYPT 2,400 BCE

B. OVER TWO THOUSAND YEARS *LATER... THE GRECO-ROMAN, CHRISTIAN-JUDEO *C.O.PY.
(*REWORKED FROM THE ANCIENT EGYPTIAN ORIGINALS)

"I, Jesus, have sent my angel to you with this testimony for the churches. I am the root and the offspring of David, [AND] THE BRIGHT M.O.R.N.I.N.G. S.T.A.R."

Rev 22:16. 1st Century CE, ie. 'A.D.'
NEW TESTAMENT - THE BIBLE

42.

A. THE ANCIENT EGYPTIAN O.R.I.G.I.N.A.L

"Behold N.(ie. 'Osiris'), HIS F.E.E.T. SHALL BE K.I.S.S.E.D."

Utterance 685. v.871b.
THE PYRAMID TEXTS
ANCIENT EGYPT 2,400 BCE

B. OVER TWO THOUSAND YEARS *LATER... THE GRECO-ROMAN, CHRISTIAN-JUDEO *C.O.P.Y.
(*REWORKED FROM THE ANCIENT EGYPTIAN ORIGINAL):

"... and did wipe [them] with the hairs of her head, and K.I.S.S.E.D. HIS F.E.E.T."

Luke 7:38. 1st Century CE, ie. 'A.D.'
NEW TESTAMENT - THE BIBLE

43.

A. THE ANCIENT EGYPTIAN O.R.I.G.I.N.A.L

""You shall reach the sky as O.R.I.O.N."

Utterance 412. v.723
THE PYRAMID TEXTS
ANCIENT EGYPT 2,400 BCE

B. OVER ONE THOUSAND YEARS *LATER... THE GRECO-ROMAN, CHRISTIAN-JUDEO *C.O.P.I.E.S.
(*REWORKED FROM THE ANCIENT EGYPTIAN ORIGINALS):

"Seek him] that maketh the seven stars and O.R.I.O.N."

Amos 5:8. 8th Century B.C.E.
OLD TESTAMENT - THE BIBLE

44.

A. THE ANCIENT EGYPTIAN O.R.I.G.I.N.A.L

"I live BY G.R.A.C.E. ..."

Utterance 570. v.1451
THE PYRAMID TEXTS
ANCIENT EGYPT 2,400 BCE

B. OVER TWO THOUSAND YEARS *LATER... THE GRECO-ROMAN, CHRISTIAN-JUDEO *C.O.P.Y.
(*REWORKED FROM THE ANCIENT EGYPTIAN ORIGINAL):

"BY G.R.A.C.E. are ye saved"

Ephesians 2:8. 1st Century CE, ie. 'A.D.'
NEW TESTAMENT - THE BIBLE

45.

A. THE ANCIENT EGYPTIAN O.R.I.G.I.N.A.L

"thou art honoured, thou art P.R.E.E.M.I.N.E.N.T., thou art a soul, thou art mighty for ever and ever."

Utterance 364. v.621c
THE PYRAMID TEXTS
ANCIENT EGYPT 2,400 BCE

B. THE GRECO-ROMAN, CHRISTIAN-JUDEO C.O.P.Y.

"And he is the head of the body, the church: who is the beginning, the firstborn from the dead; that in all
[things] he might have the P.R.E.E.M.I.N.E.N.C.E."

Ephesians 2:8. 1st Century CE, ie. 'A.D.'
NEW TESTAMENT - THE BIBLE

46.

A. THE ANCIENT EGYPTIAN O.R.I.G.I.N.A.L

"N. has ASCENDED..."
"N. has F.L.O.W.N. AS A C.L.O.U.D. TO HEAVEN"

Utterance 449. v.812c.
Utterance 467. v.891b.
THE PYRAMID TEXTS
ANCIENT EGYPT 2,400 BCE

B. OVER TWO THOUSAND YEARS *LATER... THE GRECO-ROMAN, CHRISTIAN-JUDEO *C.O.P.I.E.S.
(*REWORKED FROM THE ANCIENT EGYPTIAN ORIGINALS):

"...the Son of man ASCENDING..."
" he was LIFTED UP, and a CLOUD TOOK HIM out of their sight.

John 6:61-63 1st Century CE (ie. 'A.D.')
Acts 1:9   1st Century CE (ie. 'A.D.')
NEW TESTAMENT - THE BIBLE

47.

A. THE ANCIENT EGYPTIAN O.R.I.G.I.N.A.L
"The humans (rm.tjw) hide themselves, the GODS FLY UP"
"and when the G.O.D.S. A.S.C.E.N.D.E.D. TO HEAVEN"

Utterance 302. V.459.
Utterance 519. V.1208c.
THE PYRAMID TEXTS
ANCIENT EGYPT 2,400 BCE

B. OVER ONE THOUSAND YEARS *LATER... THE GRECO-ROMAN, CHRISTIAN-JUDEO *C.O.P.Y.
(*REWORKED FROM THE ANCIENT EGYPTIAN ORIGINALS):

"I saw G.O.D.S. A.S.C.E.N.D.I.N.G. out of the earth"

1 Samuel 28:13. 1 Samuel 10:1. 6th Century B.C.E.
OLD TESTAMENT - THE BIBLE

48.

A. THE ANCIENT EGYPTIAN O.R.I.G.I.N.A.L.S.

"They have raised themselves up, those who reside in graves"
"Let them who are in their graves, arise; let them undo their bandages. Shake off the sand from thy face"

Utterance 596. V.1641a.
Utterance 662. V.1878a-1878b.
THE PYRAMID TEXTS
ANCIENT EGYPT 2,400 BCE

B. OVER ONE THOUSAND YEARS *LATER... THE GRECO-ROMAN, CHRISTIAN-JUDEO *C.O.P.I.E.S. (*REWORKED FROM THE ANCIENT EGYPTIAN ORIGINALS):

"Thy dead men shall live, together with my dead body shall they arise... and the earth shall cast out the dead."

Isaiah 26:19 8th Century B.C.E.
OLD TESTAMENT - THE BIBLE

49..

A. THE ANCIENT EGYPTIAN O.R.I.G.I.N.A.L.

"shake off thy dust; untie thy bandages. The T.O.M.B. IS O.P.E.N. FOR THEE;

Utterance 676. V.2008b. - 2009a.
THE PYRAMID TEXTS
ANCIENT EGYPT 2,400 BCE

B. OVER TWO THOUSAND YEARS *LATER... THE GRECO-ROMAN, CHRISTIAN-JUDEO *C.O.P.Y.. (*REWORKED FROM THE ANCIENT EGYPTIAN ORIGINAL):

"Mary Magdalene went to the T.O.M.B. and saw that the stone had been R.E.M.O.V.E.D. FROM THE ENTRANCE"

John 20:1   1st Century CE, ie. 'A.D.'
NEW TESTAMENT - THE BIBLE

50.

A. THE ANCIENT EGYPTIAN O.R.I.G.I.N.A.L.S

"N. has A.S.C.E.N.D.E.D. to H.E.A.V.E.N."
"Thou A.S.C.E.N.D.E.S.T. TO H.E.A.V.E.N. like Horus"
"N. has A.S.C.E.N.D.E.D. on the rain-cloud; he has D.E.S.C.E.N.D.E.D."

Utterance 449. v.812c.
Utterance 437. v.800a.
Utterance 627. v.1774a.
THE PYRAMID TEXTS
ANCIENT EGYPT 2,400 BCE

B. OVER TWO THOUSAND YEARS *LATER... THE GRECO-ROMAN, CHRISTIAN-JUDEO *C.O.P.Y.
(*REWORKED FROM THE ANCIENT EGYPTIAN ORIGINALS):

"No one has A.S.C.E.N.D.E.D. INTO H.E.A.V.E.N. but he who D.E.S.C.E.N.D.E.D. FROM H.E.A.V.E.N., the Son of
man"

John 13:13   1st Century CE, ie. 'A.D.'
NEW TESTAMENT - THE BIBLE

51.

A. THE ANCIENT EGYPTIAN O.R.I.G.I.N.A.L.

""for thou art more E.X.A.L.T.E.D. than he, in thy N.A.M.E. of "He of the E.X.A.L.T.E.D. L.A.N.D."

Utterance 356. v.581c.
THE PYRAMID TEXTS
ANCIENT EGYPT 2,400 BCE

B. OVER ONE, TO TWO THOUSAND YEARS *LATER... THE GRECO-ROMAN, CHRISTIAN-JUDEO *C.O.P.Y. (*REWORKED FROM THE ANCIENT EGYPTIAN ORIGINAL):

"Wherefore God also hath highly E.X.A.L.T.E.D. him, and given him a N.A.M.E. which is above every name"
"By the blessing of the upright the THE C.I.T.Y. IS E.X.A.L.T.E.D." (ie. "EXALTED LAND")

Philippians 2:9   1st Century CE, ie. 'A.D.' New Testament
Proverbs 11:11   Dated *traditionally circa 950 BCE Old Testament
THE BIBLE

52.

A. THE ANCIENT EGYPTIAN O.R.I.G.I.N.A.L.

"Horus has completely filled thee with his eye, in this its name of 'F.U.L.L.N.E.S.S. O.F. G.O.D."

Utterance 364. V.614d.
THE PYRAMID TEXTS
ANCIENT EGYPT 2,400 BCE

B. OVER TWO THOUSAND YEARS *LATER... THE GRECO-ROMAN, CHRISTIAN-JUDEO *C.O.P.Y. (*REWORKED FROM THE ANCIENT EGYPTIAN ORIGINAL):

"that ye might be filled with all the F.U.L.L.N.E.S.S. O.F. G.O.D."

Ephesians 3:19   1st Century CE, ie. 'A.D.'
NEW TESTAMENT - THE BIBLE

53.

A. THE ANCIENT EGYPTIAN O.R.I.G.I.N.A.L.

"and I give J.U.D.G.E.M.E.N.T. in the HEAVENS"

Utterance 254. v.289.
THE PYRAMID TEXTS
ANCIENT EGYPT 2,400 BCE

B. OVER TWO THOUSAND YEARS *LATER... THE GRECO-ROMAN, CHRISTIAN-JUDEO *C.O.P.Y.
(*REWORKED FROM THE ANCIENT EGYPTIAN ORIGINAL):

"For we must all appear before the J.U.D.G.E.M.E.N.T. seat of Christ"

2 Corinthians 5:10 (1st Century CE, ie. 'A.D.')
NEW TESTAMENT - THE BIBLE

54.

A. THE ANCIENT EGYPTIAN O.R.I.G.I.N.A.L.

"and T.H.E. L.O.R.D. O.F. P.E.A.C.E. will give you his hand"

Utterance 254. v.286.
THE PYRAMID TEXTS
ANCIENT EGYPT 2,400 BCE

B. OVER TWO THOUSAND YEARS *LATER... THE GRECO-ROMAN, CHRISTIAN-JUDEO *C.O.P.Y.
(*REWORKED FROM THE ANCIENT EGYPTIAN ORIGINAL):

"Now T.H.E. L.O.R.D. O.F. P.E.A.C.E. himself"

2 Thessalonians 3:16   1st Century CE, ie. 'A.D.'
NEW TESTAMENT - THE BIBLE

55.

A. THE ANCIENT EGYPTIAN O.R.I.G.I.N.A.L.

"for I HAVE ASSUMED A.U.T.H.O.R.I.T.Y."

Utterance 255. v.300.
THE PYRAMID TEXTS
ANCIENT EGYPT 2,400 BCE

B. OVER TWO THOUSAND YEARS *LATER... THE GRECO-ROMAN, CHRISTIAN-JUDEO *C.O.P.Y.
(*REWORKED FROM THE ANCIENT EGYPTIAN ORIGINALS)

"he taught them as ONE THAT HAD A.U.T.H.O.R.I.T.Y."

Mark 1:22. 1st Century CE, ie. 'A.D.'
NEW TESTAMENT - THE BIBLE

56.

A. THE ANCIENT EGYPTIAN O.R.I.G.I.N.A.L.

"Unas knows him, he knows his name: E.V.E.R.L.A.S.T.I.N.G.N.E.S.S. (nHH) is his name,
E.V.E.R.L.A.S.T.I.N.G.N.E.S.S..."

'The lifetime of N. is ETERNITY, its limit is E.V.E.R.L.A.S.T.I.N.G.N.E.S.S.'

Utterance 301. v.449a..

Utterance 273-274 . v.412a.
THE PYRAMID TEXTS
ANCIENT EGYPT 2,400 BCE

B. OVER ONE THOUSAND YEARS *LATER... THE GRECO-ROMAN, CHRISTIAN-JUDEO *C.O.P.I.E.S.
(*REWORKED FROM THE ANCIENT EGYPTIAN ORIGINALS):

"and his name shall be called Wonderful, Counselor, The mighty God, The E.V.E.R.L.A.S.T.I.N.G. Father...."
Isaiah 9:6 8th Century B.C.E.
OLD TESTAMENT - THE BIBLE

Collator's Afterword-

If the Greco Roman Christian Judeo biblical text contained herein this book were not plagiarized from the Pyramid text of ancient Egypt, the explicit, endless, *chronological parallels illustrated on the previous pages would not have been possible. The law of 'odds' would simply not allow for the explicit 'mirroring' of text demonstrated in this collation to the extent that I have been able to unequivocally show. After seeing the side by side comparisons of the text/verses in this book, if you still believe in the veracity and authenticity of the Bible and it's claims, and of the claims made by those who refuse to accept 'Maat' (ie 'truth') even in the pure light of the irrefutable evidence in this book; then you may want to refer yourself to John 8:32 Kings James Version. And if one should reject the knowledge of the truth one has encountered upon reading this book then I would equally refer you to Hosea 4:6. King James Version.

I set you free; free from falsehood, free from lies, historical, biblical and otherwise; and most importantly free from self imposed, self induced.. fear; the greatest poison of all. May your relationship with God, by whatever name it reveals itself to you, be one established by yourself, free from the ignorance of others. If you cannot worship God in truth, if such be your need, then you are incapable of worshiping God, at all.

Africa has given so much to the world, it is time to give her back her credit.

Germain-Khepera, Kmt... I love you, with the same strength I have loved my mother, and that is an incomparable love. You are each the truth in my life.

The churches, the synagogues and mosques must now teach the truth, or forever close their doors.

It is done.

Eternally Black, African and Proud, in the Spirit of Love and Strength, Not Hate and Weakness...

Shakka Ahmose, child of the Nile Valley.

Harlem, New York City August 5th 2014

Bible's Textual Origin
Collated By

SHAKKA
AHMOSE

Made in the USA
Columbia, SC
14 August 2018